Blood on its hands?

Blood on its hands?

The Church and LGBT Youth

Dr Carol A Shepherd

With foreword by
Anthony Venn-Brown OAM

Dr Carol A Shepherd

Dr Carol A Shepherd is an academic, public speaker and author from Eastleigh, near Southampton, UK. As well as an experienced conference speaker, both on the academic and Christian circuit, she is the author of several academic books and papers on LGBT and faith, as well as several works of fiction. She is a global expert in the field of bisexual Christian identities. Further details of Carol's research, as well as further titles from Easy Yoke Publishing, can be found at www.easyyoke.org

You can also find details of Carol's fictional output at www.carolshepherdbooks.info

Blood on its Hands? is intended to be a good value, tell-it-like-it-is, shareable resource for all those outraged at the Western Christian Church's treatment of LGBT people. Buy it for your friends, your family, your pastor.

"Carol Shepherd was the breakout success of this conference and I would thoroughly recommend any conference or group that wants to know more about bisexuality and Christianity should invite her to come and talk."

(LGBTQ Faith UK)

"She is hilarious, engaging & tremendously sincere."

(Diverse Church)

"Fantastically witty, insightful and funny keynote from Carol Shepherd, discussing the silence towards bisexuality in the church and in LGBTQ+ organisations."

(Gathering Voices 2019)

Anthony Venn-Brown

Anthony Venn-Brown is the founder and CEO of Ambassadors & Bridge Builders International (ABBI). A former Assemblies of God evangelist, Anthony was also involved with the Christian Life Centre in Australia, the predecessor of the internationally renowned Hillsong Church.

Anthony resigned from church leadership in 1991 on coming out as a gay man. His brutally frank account of his struggles to reconcile his faith and sexuality, as well as his experiences at the hands of the ex-gay ministry, feature in his 2004 autobiography *A Life of Unlearning - Coming out of the church, One Man's Struggle.* A revised edition, *A Life of Unlearning - a Journey to Find the Truth* was published in 2007. Anthony was recently awarded the Order of Australia (OAM) for services to the LGBT+ community.

Foreword

by Anthony Venn-Brown

For years now I've been reminding people that the enemy is not individuals, churches, conversion 'therapy' organisations or advocates, or political parties; the enemy is ignorance. Change is created by focusing our energies on overcoming the latter instead of attacking the former. *Blood on its Hands?* focuses on overcoming ignorance.

This book is a winning combination of several things. Firstly, the author is an academic which means there is a commitment to research, referencing and facts, as opposed to opinion. Secondly, Dr Carol Shepherd is a writer, not only of academic works but also fiction, making this work accessible to the average reader and not written in academic speak. Thirdly, she has personal experience to draw on, being a bisexual Christian who has had to personally navigate the internal and external conflicts of faith and sexuality. Finally, the many years of research in this area have given the author additional insights and others' stories to share.

The subject of the book, the harm, and particularly the suicide of lesbian, gay, bisexual, transgender and queer (LGBTQ) people in faith contexts, is not new to many of us. I've been receiving emails and hearing similar stories since my autobiography was first published in 2004. Stories that horrified me and often brought me to tears as people shared their journeys, many for the first time, which frequently included details of their thoughts of suicide and attempts. Or the suicide of friends or family members. So many stories in fact, in order to cope, one can become desensitised to the horror of so many devastated lives.

When I first began doing media interviews in the early 2000s, every time I mentioned suicide of LGBTQ people of faith I'd become increasingly familiar with, I was either shut down or the interviewer changed the subject. The "expert" belief, at that time, was that mentioning suicide produced copy-cat deaths. I'm glad that has changed. I regret not pushing back then, but I was the new kid on the block. What would I know?

For many, the content of this book will be challenging. Finish it. Be informed. Be educated. Unless of course you find it triggering and putting you in a dark place. My experience over several decades has shown that LGBTQ people from faith backgrounds are one of the highest risk groups in our community in several key areas; three being suicide ideation, attempts and suicide itself. This is yet to be addressed not only by the church BUT the

LGBTQ community as well.

Most importantly, share it. Buy extra copies to give away strategically. Share your thoughts on social media.

I mentioned in my opening paragraph that "the enemy is ignorance." There are two types of ignorance. One is the ignorance which comes from not knowing or understanding and the other is wilful ignorance. The wilful ignorance of those who refuse to explore the possibility that they may be wrong about sexual orientation and gender identity. They never move outside their Christian bubble of websites and books which only reinforce their outdated beliefs.

Wilful ignorance is inexcusable. It is founded in prejudice and bigotry. It is usually a waste of time sharing this information with those people. There is not a binary model of those for LGBTQ equality on one side and those against on the other - it's a spectrum. It's the moveable middle, those who are questioning, that will benefit most from reading this book. They will shift, once confronted with the reality and their hearts touched. They might even move beyond just being accepting and affirming and become advocates; now armed with a new insight into our worlds, compassion, and a desire to end the horror.

Others, who have a belief in life after death and a time of judgment, and who've willingly refused to listen to our stories, will horrifyingly discover that they do have blood on their hands, and as Jesus said six times in the book of Matthew, there will be "weeping and gnashing of teeth."

Now is the time to create change. For some, tomorrow will be too late.

Chapter 1

Blood on their hands

The 2014 suicide of teenager Lizzie Lowe in a churchyard in Manchester[1] sent shockwaves around the Anglican community in the UK.

Lizzie, a regular churchgoer, had been struggling to reconcile her Christian faith with same sex attraction. Her loving parents and church leaders had no idea of Lizzie's internal battle. She had been too scared to discuss her feelings.

If any positives emerged from this tragic incident, it was the renewed vigour with which the church in question, St James & Emmanuel, Didsbury, set about bringing LGBT+ issues to the table, under the dedicated leadership of the Reverend Nick Bundock. It became an Inclusive Church[2], expanding on a programme to educate both its congregants and the wider population on the perils of ignorance when it comes to young LGBT people.

---

[1] See https://www.manchestereveningnews.co.uk/news/teenager-found-hanged-after-fears-8299328
[2] See https://www.inclusive-church.org/

Sadly, Lizzie's story is mirrored around the world. If such a tragedy can happen in the UK, considered broadly tolerant of LGBT people, then we can only begin to imagine how desperate is the plight faced by lesbian, gay, bisexual and transgender youth in less accommodating corners of the globe – and we will be looking at one of these stories in the next chapter.

However, atrocities committed in the name of religion within the Western Christian Church are my area of interest at this point in time. The truth of the matter is, as I have uncovered in my own research (Shepherd 2017, 2018, 2020), the church – in the west at least – kills largely not by stoning or other rudimentary *Handmaid's Tale*-esque methods, but by silence. Hence the next chapter is entitled *Killing them Softly*.

As in the case of Lizzie Lowe, it is the deafening silence in the church on the subject of non-heterosexual identities that causes young LGBT Christians to feel isolated and traumatised on the whole, rather than homophobic rhetoric from the pulpit. In a society where increasingly more young people do not identify as 'entirely straight' – and I will return to this in just a moment – most church leaders in the more mainstream denominations of the west know they will attract adverse reactions and headlines by engaging in anti-LGBT rhetoric.

So rather than risk besmirching the reputation of their church or religious organisation, they ignore the subject altogether. On the other hand, a more liberal stance on the part of the priest will risk upsetting more traditional factions of the church membership. In these financially and politically turbulent times, churches cannot afford to be losing paid members. The end result is the same: silence. And silence kills, as we saw in the tragic case of Lizzie Lowe.

In our church liturgies, we like to talk about sins of omission and commission. Sins of commission refer to the more obvious acts we knowingly 'commit' – perhaps not murdering or coveting our neighbour's ass, but certainly gossip, gluttony, speeding, petty theft from the stationery cupboard at work, cheating on our partner etc. Sins of omission are those things we neglect or omit to do: not helping out a friend in need, not visiting a lonely person, not challenging injustice, etc.

A YouGov poll in 2015[3] revealed that 49% of young people in the UK did not identify as 'exclusively straight.' Two years later, this figure had risen to 57% according to UK anti-bullying

---

[3] https://yougov.co.uk/topics/lifestyle/articles-reports/2015/08/16/half-young-not-heterosexual

organisation, 'Ditch the Label.'[4] In 2018, the Williams Institute at UCLA (USA) showed increased tolerance of LGBT people in its Global Acceptance Index.[5] It seems that an increasing number of young people aged 18-24 do not identify as 100% heterosexual, to the extent that non-straight identities are beginning to outstrip their straight counterparts. And an increasing percentage of the population are fully accepting of LGBT people and relationships. Yet from my own personal experience, based on some 30 years of church attendance, and the experiences of the countless research participants I have interviewed, the majority of churches still behave as if LGBT people do not exist. Youth resources coyly touch on human sexuality without going into detail, and rarely is the subject broached in sermons. Church leaders are woefully ill-equipped in this area, an issue that emerged time and time again in my own research in the UK and US (2017) and Europe (2020b). Frankly, they do not know what to do about LGBT and LGBT people, so they brush the whole issue under the carpet.

---

[4] https://www.ditchthelabel.org/research-papers/the-annual-bullying-survey-2017/

[5] https://williamsinstitute.law.ucla.edu/press/press-releases/lgbt-acceptance-increases-press-release/

Indeed, in the UK, the Church of England still adheres to a 29 year old document, *Issues in Human Sexuality* (Church of England, 1991), when it comes to training would-be priests for ministry. This statement by the House of Bishops is mandatory reading for candidates for ordination within the Anglican Church. The booklet, just 43 pages long, contains seventeen pages on what it calls 'The Phenomenon of Homosexual Love,' in which bisexual people in particular come in for some particularly short shrift. Given just a paragraph (5.8), which is 119 words long, bisexual Christians are advised to stick to their 'heterophile learnings' or seek a counsellor for their potential personality disorder! This latter point is particularly irresponsible when we consider the earlier statistics on young people's perceptions of their sexual identity, a good number of whom would potentially identify as bisexual.

In January 2020, the Church of England announced it would continue to teach that sexual relationships are only permissible within heterosexual couplings, de facto ignoring the theological input and lived experiences of several leading experts from the LGBT Christian community involved in the Living in Love and Faith talks.[6] The trend of straight people writing

---

[6] https://www.bbc.co.uk/news/newsbeat-51233003

and legislating about their non-straight brethren, with little recourse to the lived realities of the latter, continues to this day in the Church of England and within many other mainstream Christian denominations – and all of this, with little or no concern for the mental health of those individuals over which they purport to exercise pastoral care.

What many church leaders fail to understand is that LGBT Christians face a unique sense of adverse circumstances, linked to being neither accepted by the secular LGBT Community on the basis of their faith, nor accepted by church communities on account of their sexuality. This 'surround sound' of disapproving noise in the form of multiple micro-aggressions leads to what sociologist Illyan Meyer termed 'minority stress' (Meyer, 2003). What many also fail to grasp – unless confronted by the issue closer to home – is that same-sex attracted people or those with non-binary sexual orientations or gender identities **do not have a choice** in the matter. *Nobody* wakes up and says: "I know, I'm going to make my life 100% more difficult by becoming queer." LGBT people are not lying about how they feel and experience the world!

Consider the following from Lucy Knight, writing in the Guardian newspaper in 2019[7]:

---

[7] https://www.theguardian.com/commentisfree/2019/mar/21/gay-christian-church-lgbt

… even when I'm 90% sure the person I'm addressing will be accepting, I still get that little jerky stomach-knot right before I say the words "gay" or "girlfriend" to someone new. Growing up in the church has played quite a big part in these insecurities. The ultimate lowlight was confiding in a pastor about my sexuality when I was 18. He politely informed me that my feelings were from the devil and went on to share our conversation – which I had believed to be confidential – with the church the following Sunday as part of his sermon on "sexual immorality". There was also the church member who arranged to meet me for coffee in order to say I needed to repent; and the friend who bought me a book on "conversion therapy" for Christmas. I could go on. Most LGBT+ Christians I've come across have similar stories to tell, if not worse.

As a researcher in this area, I have come across dozens of stories of this ilk, and just a small proportion of these are featured in Chapter 2,

Killing them Softly and Chapter 4, *Con-version Therapy.* It is small wonder therefore that the mental health statistics for LGBT Christians make for grim reading.

Mental Health & LGBT people

Let us consider first some sobering statistics around mental health and LGBT people in general. There are numerous studies which show the disproportionate psychological distress suffered by non-heterosexual people compared to their heterosexual peers. I've highlighted just a few of them here. A trawl through any leading search engine will reveal a great many more, with Google Scholar offering a whole host of academic papers on this subject.

For example, back in 2010, a Canadian Public Health Survey (Brennan et al., 2010) found that lesbian and gay people are twice as likely to take their own lives as straight people (see Table 1.1), with the bisexual cohort of the LGBT community *six* times more likely.

Bisexual mental health is an area all by itself; bisexual people face a unique set of mental health impactors due to rejection from the straight and lesbian and gay communities alike. Bisexual people may be subject to either 'bi erasure' – censorship of bisexual issues in the interests of lesbian and gay sexual politics, or 'biphobia' – irrational fear of bisexual people, based on erroneous notions that all bisexual people sleep around, eternally cheat on one gender for another, etc.

Table 1.1: Suicidality among LGB men and women in Canada, 2010

Sexual Orientation	Suicidality Among Women		Suicidality Among Men	
	Percentage	Adjusted rate (Compared to heterosexual)	Percentage	Adjusted rate (Compared to heterosexual)
Bisexual	45.40%	5.9	34.80%	6.3
Lesbian/Gay	29.50%	3.5	25.20%	4.1
Heterosexual	9.60%	-	7.40%	-

Source: San Francisco Human Rights Commission, *Bisexual Invisibility: Impacts & Recommendations* (SFHRC, 2011a)

I have written extensively on bisexual issues, particularly within a Christian context, and am one of the global experts in this area of bisexual Christian identities, along with Andrew Yip and Alex Toft in the UK and Margaret Robinson in Canada. For more reading in this area, I direct you to Bisexuality in the Western Christian Church: The damage of silence (Shepherd, 2018) and Bisexuality, Religion and Spirituality: Critical Perspectives by Andrew Yip & Alex Toft (2020a). My forthcoming book, *Bi the Way: Pastoring Bisexual Christians in Europe* (Shepherd, 2020b), contains interviews with bisexual Christians around the European continent, from the UK in the West to Russia in the East. For an eminently readable and good value trade book on the bisexual Christian experience, I recommend Jaime Sommers' 2016 autobiography, <u>119: My Life as a Bisexual Christian</u> (Sommers, 2016).

Meanwhile, a study published in 2020 by the American Academy of Paediatrics (AAP)[8], revealed that LGBT youth were more than three times as likely to attempt suicide than their straight peers. Data was taken from six US states between 2009 and 2017 and found that, although the number of suicide attempts among LGBT people under the age of 18 had decreased over the eight-year period, they still remained more than three times as likely to try to take their own lives than the straight cohort. In 2009, 26.7% of queer youth reported a suicide attempt within the previous twelve months, compared with 6.3% of their straight counterparts. In 2017, it still high at 20.1%, compared with 5.9% of straight youth.

The trend continues in Australia, with figures from the <u>National LGBTI Alliance Report of 2020</u>

---

[8] See <u>https://www.pinknews.co.uk/2020/03/04/lgbt-suicide-youth-study-sexual-minority-american-academy-pediatrics-samaritans/</u>

revealing that, compared to the general population, LGBTI people are more likely to attempt suicide in their lifetime:

- young people aged 16 to 27 are five times more likely
- transgender people aged 18 and over are nearly eleven times more likely
- People with an intersex variation aged 16 and over are nearly six times more likely
- LGBT young people who experience abuse and harassment are more likely to attempt suicide

LGBT Christian Mental Health

In terms of LGBT *Christian* mental health, Gibbs & Goldbach (2015) of the University of Southern California have written on religious conflict in LGBT Christian young people. They investigated the effect of minority stress on LGBT suicidality, using a large sample of around three thousand participants. The main findings from this study were that LGBT young adults who leave the church for self-acceptance reasons were more at risk of suicide. This was due to a loss of support systems, despite gains in personal freedom. In short:

- LGBT young adults who experience religious identity conflict are at significant risk of suicide.
- LGBT Christians experience better outcomes when involved in LGBT affirming faith communities than when not attending church at all.

Anthony Venn-Brown of Australian organisation, Ambassadors and Bridge Builders International (ABBI) has also reported on the elevated suicide rates of LGBT people of faith. Summarising findings from the research project, *Writing Themselves in 3* (WTi3), which interviewed 3134 LGBT young people aged from 14-21 in 2010, Venn-Brown writes:

> ...LGBT people of faith and religion experience the usual issues of resolving their sexuality or gender identity, coming out, finding their place in the community and learning what it means to live authentically in a predominately straight world. They often, however, experience these things with greater intensity and also have additional issues to deal with

making them potentially one of the highest risk groups in our community.

When religion was mentioned the key findings were:

1. More likely to feel bad about their same sex attraction.
2. More likely to have experienced social exclusion or had to tolerate homophobic language from friends.
3. More likely to report homophobic abuse in the home.
4. More likely to report feeling unsafe at home.
5. More likely to not be supported by their mother, father, brother, teacher or student welfare coordinator/counsellor, when disclosing their SSA.
6. More likely to report thoughts of self-harm and suicide or to carry out self-harm.[9]

My own research into bisexual Christian identities (Shepherd, 2018) revealed the following disturbing statistics:- of 54 bisexual Christians interviewed in the UK and USA, 93% reported depressive symptoms, ranging from anxiety and

---

[9] See https://www.abbi.org.au/2012/04/gay-religious-suicide/

depression to suicide ideation or suicide attempts. *Only four (7%) reported no depressive symptoms at all.*

Another survey by a research team based at the University of West Virginia again found a direct link between queer Christians and increased suicidality – thought interestingly *not* among bisexual Christians, in contrast to previous studies. An article written by Anne Harding on Reuters in April 2018 notes[10]:

> Although religiosity is generally tied to reduced suicide risk, the opposite may be true for some young lesbian, gay and questioning adults, researchers say. Based on data from more than 21,000 U.S. college students, researchers found that greater religious feeling and engagement was tied to increased risk of suicidal thoughts and actions for participants who identified as LGBQ.
>
> "Religion has typically been seen as something that would protect somebody from thoughts of suicide or trying to kill themselves, and in our study our evidence suggests that may not be the

---

[10] https://uk.reuters.com/article/us-health-lgbq-religion-suicide/religious-faith-linked-to-suicidal-behavior-in-lgbq-adults-idUKKBN1HK2MA

case for everyone, particularly for those we refer to as sexual minority people," said one of the study authors, John Blosnich of the Injury Control Research Center at West Virginia University in Morgantown.

Previous research suggests that belonging to a religious faith reduces risky behaviour in young people, such as substance use and unsafe sex, Blosnich noted in a telephone interview. Religiosity has also been linked to a lower risk of suicidal behaviours, but there is some evidence to suggest that the impact of religion may be different for lesbian, gay, bisexual and questioning (LGBQ) individuals.

The study team analysed survey data from the 2011 University of Texas at Austin's Research Consortium on 21,247 college-enrolled 18- to 30-year-olds, including 2.3 percent who reported being lesbian or gay, 3.3 percent who identified as bisexual and 1.1 percent who were questioning their sexuality.

All participants rated the importance of religion in their lives on a 1 to 5 scale, from "not important" to "very important." Between 21 percent and 28 percent of LGBQ participants rated the importance of religion to them at a 4 or 5, compared with 39 percent of heterosexuals, researchers report in American Journal of Preventive Medicine.

Questioning youth had the highest rate of recent thoughts about suicide, at 16.4 percent, compared with 3.7 percent of heterosexuals, 6.5 percent of lesbian/gay individuals and 11.4 percent of bisexuals. Lifetime suicide attempts were reported by 20 percent of bisexual youth, 17 percent of questioning youth, 14 percent of gay or lesbian youth and 5 percent of heterosexuals.

For bisexual youth, the importance of religion was not associated with suicidal behaviour, while religiosity was protective against thoughts of suicide and suicidal attempts in the heterosexual youth. But lesbians and gays who reported that religion was important to them were 38 percent more likely to have had recent suicidal thoughts. For lesbians only, religion was associated with a 52 percent increased likelihood of suicidal thinking.

Questioning individuals were almost three times as likely to have attempted suicide recently if they reported that religion was very important to them.

Among lesbians and gays who said religion was not important to them, there was no association between sexual orientation and recent suicide attempts. But being homosexual did significantly increase the likelihood of recent suicide attempts in people who said that religion was very important to them.

"Some sexual minority folks are really at odds. They feel very confused or they feel that they are in conflict with their faith because of who they are. That's a very scary place to be in," Blosnich said.

"We are definitely not saying that religion, period, is bad; it's not," he added. "There are many sexual minority people who find great strength and great sources of support in their religious communities, but unfortunately we hear many stories about people who do not."

To place all of these figures quoted in the various studies in perspective, statistics published online by MIND (2016)[11] and Mental Health America (2015)[12] suggest that one in four UK adults (25%) and one in five US adults (20%) suffer from mental health problems at any one time, regardless of their sexual orientation. In Australia, the figure also stands at one in five.[13] It is clear that something is going badly wrong with both the attitude we hold towards, or the pastoral support we offer, LGBT Christians if they are 4-6 times more likely to take their own lives than straight Christians.

You may disagree, but it is no exaggeration, in my opinion, to conclude that the Christian Church has blood on its hands – all this without stoning LGBT people to death or indeed even laying a finger on them.

In what sense are we killing young people, for an orientation they can almost certainly do absolutely nothing about (without even going into why they should want to, anyway)? This will be explored in the following chapters.

---

[11] See https://www.mind.org.uk
[12] See https://https://www.mhanational.org/
[13] See https://www.healthdirect.gov.au

Chapter 2

Killing them Softly

I stated at the end of the last chapter that we don't stone or execute LGBT people in the developed world. I am going to begin this chapter, however, by sharing a harrowing story from Iraq.

As well as a college lecturer and writer, I am also the secretary of an international LGBT faith organisation. Pleas for humanitarian aid come into my inbox on a regular basis. Sometimes the stories I hear break my heart. This is one of them. I have changed her name and local place names to protect her identity and tidied up the English slightly, though trying to keep it in her own words as far as possible.

I would also just like to preface her letter by stating that my purpose in sharing this communication is *not* to denigrate Islam. Like Christianity, Islam is at its heart a peace-loving religion practised largely by peace-loving people. This is rather about what happens when we misuse God and sacred Scriptures for our own ends and our own political goals.

Dear Madam/Sir,

My name is Abida. I'm a 23 year old lesbian girl from Baghdad, Iraq. I would be thankful if you can read my letter.

I'm from a fanatical Muslim family. My father's relationship with my mother and me was very bad since my childhood. He used to beat us if we just expressed our opinions. During the fall of Baghdad in 2003, my family travelled outside Baghdad to the region where my mother and father come from. We stayed with my mother's family, in a closed community with Bedouin traditions.

I started going to a school for girls only. When I was studying, my father used to beat me and tear my books and say a girl's place is in the kitchen and when the girl grows up, her duty is to serve her husband! My father forced me to be absent from school, but my young teacher visited us and she convinced him to return me back to my classes. Following this incident, I started to feel admiration and love towards my teacher but I hid my feelings because it's forbidden in the Muslim restricted community where I live. Every day I went to school, I brought her a flower to show her my feelings, but she considered me just a child who liked her favourite teacher! I told my mother that I loved my teacher and I liked girls that I had no feelings for boys. My mum started to beat me and threatened to tell my father, then he would kill me. She warned me that love is only for parents, God, the Prophet Muhammad, and sexual feelings are only for the husband. When the situation in Baghdad improved, my father decided to return to our house in Baghdad. I became very sad, because I would be away from my kind teacher.

Years later, my tendencies began to increase towards females. I did not share my girlfriends at school's interest in male actors or male celebrities; on the contrary, I was attracted to female celebrities. At the age of 15, I tried to escape from the house. Although I was a teenager, I wanted to escape from this unbearable pressure, but my father saw me while I was leaving the house with a backpack, so my father and my mother and my only brother beat me, then my father locked me in the house for six months. I couldn't get out of my room! After this isolation, humiliation and confinement at home with me begging and apologizing to my father, he agreed that I could return to school, on the condition that my brother followed me and returned me home, and that I promised him not to repeat it.

One day my mother asked me about my opinions on marriage, so I told her frankly this time that I'm a lesbian and I don't have any interest in men, only girls. So she realised that I hadn't changed since my youth and she ran to my father and told him that I was a bitch, because a lesbian is a bitch in their minds and I shouldn't live there. It was a good excuse for my father to torture me again. They were creative in torturing and hurting me, and this time, more brutally. They forced me to have an operation to cut the clitoris - female genital mutilation or FGM – at the age of seventeen. After this painful operation, I was really broken and in a deep psychological distress and real pain and I

decided to run away from home. This time I was successful,
I did it!

I ran away and stayed temporarily with a Christian friend
for two weeks. She was studying with me and they moved
to another district of Baghdad which is predominantly Shiaa
and Christian. It was far away from the predominantly
Sunni district where my family lives. I asked her if I could
stay for several days until I organised my escape from Iraq.
Her family sympathized with me after they saw the signs of
my torture, especially my operation, my female genital
mutilation, which I showed to my friend's mother. I told my
friend that I was a lesbian. She said she was straight but she
understood me and she reassured me this is an ordinary
instinct, not a crime, as the Islamic religion claims!

During the days I spent with them, I found out that the
Christian religion is a religion of love, not like Islam, which
is a religion for men to satisfy their instincts, where women in
the Islamic religion must be under male command and be
obedient to their husbands and fulfil all his sexual demands.
My relationship with my friend's Christian family
strengthened. I was praying with them and started reading
the Bible. My friend gifted me a cross, which did not leave
my chest! This cross filled me with a sense of relief! I wish I
could change my religion completely in public, but Iraqi law
does not allow that.

I left their house to make my way to the airport.
Unfortunately, my family reported me to all Baghdad police
stations, and the police caught me. They put me in a detention

room, they harassed me and tried to rape me, which exacerbated my feelings towards men. The police released me, when my family arrived to collect me. My father took me to our house and my greatest tragedy started there. My brother beat me and broke my wrist, while my father tied my feet with iron chains and beat me very hard with a belt. Then I was thrown into a dark room that was used as a warehouse without going to the bathroom. I was treated in an inhumane way and given crumbs to eat. After twenty days of this prison, beating and humiliation, my father stipulated that he would undo my chains and return me to life, on condition that I have to get married. I didn't want that, but I agreed only to get out of this painful prison and torture.

I thought it was a threat only, but when I finished my studies at high school, and after the last exam, I was shocked when my father sent me my unknown husband's house. He forced me to get married. I was raped from day one and I didn't have any feelings for this person who turned out to be the servant in the mosque where my father prays. My life with this husband was another tragedy and another hell. After a few months, I discovered that I was pregnant. I told him that I didn't want the child and I wouldn't tend to him as a husband because I'm a lesbian. I hoped that he would understand me and divorce me, but he beat me, tortured me, locked me up and put me on a bed in his room. He told me that I'm here as an animal until I give birth to his son. A 9 months of pregnancy, I gave birth to his baby. He started to beat me again and told me he won't stop until I die. The family took me and threw me in the garage like garbage. My father punched my face and broke my tooth because I'm a burden and shameful. I stayed as a pariah with my family for a year and I was treated so badly because of the shame of me being a lesbian, which meant my husband would divorce me and bring huge shame to the family, in their words.

I started to write to a lawyer and told her about my case and I asked her to file for divorce from my husband. He did not agree to divorce me so my lawyer filed for "Khula" - which is a divorce in return for compensation to be paid by the wife to her husband. I won the case after I gave up all my rights like alimony etc. I gave up everything to earn my freedom. I'm a human being, created free and I don't subscribe to these barbaric traditions and backwards Islamic society.

This time I successfully escaped from my family and all these people who hurt me and now I live in female student housing. I have an admin job but I can't go out because I would be in severe danger of being killed by my father or brother or even my ex-husband. I live in a country that rape women's rights. Women in Iraq are powerless without a deterrent law protecting us. I would like to move to a safe place where homosexuals will not be killed and tortured and is not racist, a place where a person can choose his way of life and religion! Please help me to move to your safe country, where homosexuals are people, not outcasts, and can live in peace without abuse and fear. Jesus bless you.

Clearly this is distressing in the extreme. Reading this letter was upsetting enough, let alone being the one suffering at the hands of such inhumanity. Unfortunately, I had to explain to Abida that we were not a humanitarian aid society; we had limited resources and all we could do was uphold her in prayer, which we have done.

As I said earlier, I tell this story not to denigrate Islam. I know from Muslim friends and acquaintances, that Islam is at its core a peaceful religion. And there are LGBT faith organisations for Christians and Muslims alike. There are queer Christians, queer Muslims, queer Jews and queer Sikhs who have reconciled their faiths with their sexuality. Worship communities and groups exist if you are queer and practise any of these world faiths. You don't have to feel alone in the UK, though I cannot speak for other countries.

However, the sad thing about Abida's story, apart from the terrible torture and suffering she has endured, is that hatred and torture of LGBT people are not restricted to strict Islamic cultures. Whilst international law in the Western largely prevents such torrid physical abuse from taking place, hatred and psychological abuse of young LGBT people still occurs on a regular basis in our Christian churches and religious communities. Sadly, this trend is becoming more prevalent again in these times of retrogressive, right-wing policies in much of Eastern Europe, Eurasia and the United States, with the mushrooming of LGBT-free zones in Poland and violence against LGBT people in Russia just two cases in point. Without seeking in any respect to minimise the horrors of physical torture compounded with mental torture, seen to particularly distressing effect in Chechnya, the more insidious cumulative effect of micro-aggressions leave life-long scars on LGBT people, too.

LGBT Christian experiences in the UK and US

I want to consider now some experiences of LGBT Christians rather closer to home. As I said at the start, I am an academic researcher as well as a writer, and I have done considerable research in the area of LGBT Christian identities. A large chunk of my output focuses on the serious implications of ignorance and silence concerning LGBT issues on the mental health of queer youth. I'm going to read to you now some accounts from UK and US young people.

The first is from Melissa, a 19 year old from the States:

When I first recognised my feelings of a same-sex attraction to someone, my anxiety and depression began. I knew that I wasn't in control of my attraction and that scared me, especially when thinking about how God, the world, my family, and my friends would view me.

I had the belief that I was a sinner because of my sexuality and that I would go to Hell. I tried so hard to hold back and deny myself of this attraction, but it made my anxiety and depression so much worse. I pleaded to God and asked 'Why me?' over and over and I didn't know what to do.

One day I just realised that God wants me to be happy. He doesn't want me to hate myself, or hold back who I truly am, or want to die. So I finally accepted myself and the anxiety and depression went away for a while… until I told my mom about my same-sex relationship.

Her reaction and negative words affected me and hurt me so badly that the anxiety and depression came back even stronger and continued to worsen over time. I experienced self-hate, obsessive thoughts, constant worry and deep depression.

My body physically changed as well. I often got nauseous and would throw up regularly when my anxiety got so bad. I developed an eating disorder in which I could not eat without throwing up and I lost 15 pounds. I became very weak and gloomy, feeling dread every day. I tried an anti-anxiety medication, Lexapro, and after taking it for three days, I had the worse anxiety attack I have ever experienced and voluntarily admitted myself to a psychiatric hospital for three days.

During these three days, I was able to heal many of the wounds that I had felt for the past five months since coming out to my mom.

The second account is from Amelia, aged 35, from Manchester, UK, who is describing why she left the church as a young woman:

I was being told very clearly and strongly that God thinks this [homosexuality] is a sin. I felt it was a choice between… believing in the kind of God I wanted to believe in, who was loving and just, or agreeing with Church that being gay is sinful. And I left, because I couldn't reconcile those two things. At the time I left, my belief in God was still quite strong… without a church community, I gradually lost my faith in God and that was very distressing and very upsetting at the time. It was a really, really big part of my life and I felt driven out… A lot of people suggested that I'd drifted away – I felt driven out.

A number of those I interviewed in the USA and UK mentioned suicide ideation. Tristan, a young student from the UK commented:

I have attempted suicide twice… part of it is definitely linked to faith and sexuality… it has affected a lot of my self-belief, self-esteem.'

I will touch on more of these interviews in Chapter 4, *Con-Version Therapy*.

Sadly, many other young people *have* taken their own life, due to the perceived irresolvable conflict between their faith and sexuality. Again, I believe it is no exaggeration to claim church leaders have blood on their hands, in those cases where these young people did not receive the due care and diligence they should have been offered as vulnerable young people, irrespective of the religious views of the incumbent priest or youth leader.

The Tyler Clementi case

In 2010, a spate of teenage suicides among the LGBT community in the United States received a great deal of media coverage and debate among clergy. Whilst direct links could not be established with any particular church fellowship, it was clear that the bullying and harassment that these youths were subjected to, was the result of living and studying in conservative religious environments.

Of the five suicides that rocked America in autumn 2010, the most notorious was that of Tyler Clementi, an 18 year old first year student at Rutgers University, New Jersey. Clementi threw himself off the George Washington Bridge having been filmed and livestreamed having a sexual encounter with another man by his so-called friends. Clementi's death prompted the *It Gets Better* campaign on college campuses, aimed at supporting and encouraging young LGBT people that life improves as you mature, and not to despair. Sadly, the campaign came too late for Clementi and the other four young people who took their own lives.

Clementi's death also prompted his mother, Jane, to set up the Tyler Clementi Foundation in his name, an organisation which aims to educate and support parents of LGBT children. In a freely available interview with the Huffington Post in November 2018[14], Jane Clementi calls on parents and church leaders to come to a new understanding of God's diverse creation:

Losing My Gay Son To Suicide Changed the Way I View My Christian Faith *by Jane Clementi*

To try and change what God has created causes significant harm.

---

[14] See https://www.huffpost.com/entry/gay-son-christianity_n_5b466516e4b022fdcc557ce1?ncid=engmodushpmg0 0000006

Like all my children, my son Tyler had red hair. Red hair is pretty rare — only around two percent of the world's population is born with it. In fact, Tyler was born with many of my traits. Everywhere I go, people tell me how much he looked like me.

There were many traits he was born with, like his hair colour and his amazing gifts as a musician. Music was an inborn trait that just called to him from an early age. It was his passion and a deep part of who he was.

There were other traits that he was not born with, traits that I encouraged and helped to instil in him: doing well in school, being a caring brother and a thoughtful friend. I shared my faith with him by bringing him to church, hoping to instil in him the values that I believed in and surrounding him with a community that loved and cared for our family.

Tyler was the sum of all these parts and more, both his nature and his nurture. He was a vibrant, intelligent and talented young man. He died by suicide when he was 18, after he was viciously cyberbullied on his college campus. And what breaks my heart is that I believe Tyler was bullied because he was gay, another God-given trait he was born with. Who Tyler loved was as unchangeable as his bright, natural hair colour, and another person used that to humiliate him and crush his spirit.

I'm a different person now than I was before my son died. Losing the child whose features I shared, whose hand I held, whose homework I checked and whose violin recitals I attended fundamentally changed the way I see the world.

I understand bullying and the devastation it can cause differently as well. And as a mother who brought her son up in a Christian community and later lost him to suicide, I want to speak to every parent who wishes they could change a trait that was given to their child by God.

I was again reminded of the important role organized religion can play in shaping how our children view themselves when I previewed an important film that opened this weekend called "Boy Erased." Based on the memoir by Garrard Conley, the film tells the courageous story of the son of a Baptist pastor in a small American town who must overcome the fallout of being outed to his parents. His parents struggle to reconcile their love for their son with their beliefs. Fearing a loss of family, friends and community, the young man is pressured into attending a conversion therapy program.

Telling your child or letting a religious leader tell your child that there is something wrong with them because of who they love is bullying. A church community that treats your child as being broken, less than or separated from God because they are gay or lesbian or bisexual, and insists that they must be fixed or repaired, is bullying. Sending your child to so-called reparative therapy is as damaging and traumatic as a beating from the schoolyard bully. None of it will change your child who is gay or lesbian.

To try and change what God has created causes significant harm. Reparative therapy can cause depression, anxiety, drug use, homelessness and suicidal ideation. It has been rejected by every mainstream medical and mental health organization as a dangerous and fraudulent practice that is traumatic and psychologically painful.

It is simply foolishness to continue to read Scripture with eyes of the first century. We must use all the knowledge and wisdom God continues to give to us today, in the 21st century. God has shown us through research that we cannot change a person's sexual orientation, just as we have learned that red hair and blue eyes are determined by your genes and are unchangeable.

Since the day I lost my son, I've changed the way I look at the teachings and traditions of the Christian church, and I now belong to a faith community that affirms all people just as God created them.

I also recognized that above all else, Christians are called to love. We have been told that love is patient and kind. Love always protects, always trusts, always hopes. Love never fails us. Loving and embracing your gay, lesbian or bisexual child as God created them will never fail you. But reparative therapy will — it will fail you, and it will fail your children.

Reparative therapy will feature, as stated, in Chapter 4. But just for one moment, let us consider this: who are the 'bad guys' in these accounts, from Abida in Iraq, to Tyler Clementi in New York State?

The young people themselves?
The friends?
The parents?

The college staff?
The (absent) church leaders?
Politicians?
God?

Chapter 3

The Iron Yoke of Christ?

Most people reading this book will already be familiar with the verse from Matthew 11 v 30, where Jesus says: *Take my yoke upon you and learn from me. My yoke is easy and my burden is light.*

It is a verse that means a great deal to me; in fact, I named my publishing imprint and public speaking ministry after it. I would like you just to take a moment and read the last part of it slowly to yourself again: *My yoke is easy and my burden is light.*

It is key to the overriding message of this book, and indeed to my ethos as an LGBT Christian writer and speaker.

It is commonly agreed among reputable biblical scholars that we need to read a passage in its cultural context to understand the underlying message below the metaphor, though this rule appears to be applied more rigorously to some issues than others, with homosexuality being a case in point.

A yoke is an agricultural reference to a wooden harness which cattle, usually oxen, would wear in those days to balance the weight as they pulled the plough or another heavy load. It was designed to rest on their shoulders, so that it did not cause them too much discomfort, hence the reference to easy. (There are other types of yoke mentioned in Scripture which are less easy on the body and I will touch on those in just a bit). Usually a more experienced ox would be paired with a less experienced one - we might say a young apprentice - to support the younger ox. It also enabled the load to be spread; not all the burden fell on the shoulders of one.

Jesus clearly knew his audience would be familiar with this image. He lived in an agrarian society. In our technological society of today, we might use a different metaphor. But the underlying meaning would be the same: Jesus is with us, helping share the load. And because Jesus is strong and we are weak, he shoulders most of it. Hence, our burden is light, in comparison.

If this is the metaphor Christ himself uses, why then, do we place such ridiculous loads on the shoulders of vulnerable people, through expecting them to deny or alter something entirely out of their power to change - namely, their sexual orientation? As is often the case in our churches, the load borne is the weight of silence. Clergy - and therefore those who follow their lead - remain resolutely silent about LGBT issues, so that young people feel isolated, disproportionately burdened and too scared to talk. The heart-rending suicide of teenager Lizzie Lowe in Manchester in 2014, mentioned already in Chapter 1, should have served as huge wake up call to churches and faith leaders about the need to engage intelligently and **truthfully** with LGBT issues. Sadly this is still not the case in many mainstream denominations throughout Europe, North America and Australasia, where endless rounds of 'fact-finding' conversations, that all too often ignore the lived realities of LGBT lives and are little more than box-ticking exercises, are still the order of the day.

Lizzie Lowe was a devout Christian teenager who was too scared to tell her parents and church leaders that she was gay. These adults were perfectly decent people. It emerged that her anxieties were misplaced – but somehow Lizzie had got the message that her sexuality was shameful, that she, in her very core, was an aberration. This in itself is a tragedy. When we are silent about the reality of same sex attraction in our churches, the results can be devastating, as this example only too clearly demonstrates.

What on God's earth gives *anyone* the right to place such burdens on the shoulders of young people, let alone vulnerable young LGBT people of faith? What entitles anyone to tell young women and young men that they are wrong about who they are, that feelings that come naturally are wrong, even that they are, in the words of the Catechism of the Catholic Church, *intrinsically disordered*? Straight people, would *you* accept another person at church or in your workplace telling *you* that your inborn sexual orientation was wrong? Just take a second to honestly reflect on that question.

I said earlier that several mentions are made of yokes in the Bible. Often, however, the reference or metaphor does not relate to animal husbandry, but to bondage. In Jeremiah 28: 12-14, God's prophet Jeremiah is restricted by a wooden yoke, in order to curtail his activities, giving the false prophet, Hananiah, license to roam, spreading falsehoods to the Babylonians. But God intervenes, as we see in the Scripture:

> I left the temple, and a little while later, the LORD told me to go back and say to Hananiah: I am the LORD All-Powerful, the God of Israel. You smashed a wooden yoke, but I will replace it with one made of iron. I will put iron yokes on all the nations, and they will have to do what King Nebuchadnezzar commands. I will even let him rule the wild animals.

It is obvious that the iron yoke is a considerable step up from the wooden yoke, a complete restrictor of movement, a means of exerting total control over people. This is not the easy yoke mentioned by Jesus in our earlier passage from Matthew 11. Clearly the image is metaphorical, but an iron yoke was altogether more brutal, chafing into the neck, rather like the neck brace and chains used on black slaves in the 17th century.

Let us now go back to our young people from Chapter 2 – those who have attempted to take their own lives, and those who succeeded in their tragic mission. Was the teaching they received at church the easy yoke of Christ or the iron yoke seen here in our passage from Jeremiah?

There are generally thought to be **seven** mentions of homosexuality in the Bible, though contextual readings of Scripture cast considerable doubt on their direct application to innate homosexuality and loving same-sex relationships such as we know them today. There are considerably more passages that directly tell us to love another. I found around **fifty** straightaway on an initial search. Here's just one of them:

1 John 4:20 (English Standard Version)

If anyone says, "I love God," and hates his brother, he is a liar; for he who does not love his brother whom he has seen cannot love God whom he has not seen.

Many churches and Christian organisations, usually on the evangelical wing, like to say they are 'Bible Believing Christians'. They may pompously proclaim on their signs outside: so and so church, *a Bible believing congregation*. Yet they all too often cherry pick verses out of Scripture, with little or no recourse to its cultural context, to justify the oppression of vulnerable people in the name of righteousness. Ask anyone LGBT if they made a conscious decision to be queer, and you will get the same answer: "No, it's just the way I am, I always felt different." Some people have even tried to change, putting themselves through damaging conversion therapies, often with lifelong mental health implications and sometimes, tragically, leading them to take their own lives, as we will see in the next chapter.

Well, I'm a Bible believing Christian, too, and for me there is **absolutely nothing** in the character or ministry of Jesus Christ as outlined in the Scriptures to suggest he would treat *anyone* in the way many church leaders treat LGBT people, expecting them to deny their ontological existence. What I do see in Scripture, though, are many instances where Jesus himself 'breaks the rules' in the name of love and acceptance of the marginalised – for example, in Luke 13, where Jesus heals on the Sabbath. Indeed, it is the legalistic Pharisees, who quote Scripture and put rules before people, who come in for the sharp end of Jesus' tongue. What does that suggest Jesus would do, confronted with a conservative priest and a young gay man? Take the side of the judgemental or the loving?

If you are reading this and you are straight, I'd just like you to take a moment and ask yourself this:

When did you decide to be heterosexual?

You just *are*, right? It's not of your own proactive moral choosing. You were just born that way, and handily for you, it was the Blood Type O of sexual orientations, the most common and thereby most socially acceptable sexuality to have the good fortune to be born into – heterosexuality. Like white privilege, there is heterosexual privilege. You did not earn your straight identity by virtue or good deeds. You just had the (arguable) good fortune to be born that way.

As I discussed earlier, research is showing that over 50% of young people between 18 and 24 no longer identify as exclusively heterosexual, meaning they are somewhere on the LGBT spectrum. Yet we still live in a heteronormative society, and no more so than in most of our churches, where it is simply assumed everyone is straight. How does the mainstream Christian church think it is going to attract new young members to its dying congregations when it denies the reality of a significant proportion of potential visitors and gets the backs up of the remaining 50%, brought up on liberal 21st century values?

If you'll bear with me, I'd just like you to close your eyes for a moment and imagine this scenario. It's a parallel universe where same-sex attraction is the norm, the ruling majority. I want you to imagine you've been told *never* to act on your heterosexual feelings. If you have a partner, you need to give them up, *even* if you've been married to them for most of your adult life. If you don't have an opposite sex partner, then you need to abstain from any form of romantic or sexual human contact for the rest of your life. You must remain celibate - until you die.

I suspect that's a terrifying thought for most of you, isn't it?

Jesus said that his yoke is easy and his burden is light. He also said in John 10:10 that he came to give us life to the full, not that we shall live an empty, joyless shell of an existence by virtue of an attraction or gender identity we can do nothing about, without inflicting mental and sometimes physical torture on ourselves. Psalm 139 tells us we were designed by God before we were even born. The iron yokes we place around LGBT young people's necks when we deny their very inmost being, does not speak the Gospel to me. The burden is not light, the yoke is not easy, when we treat people in a way we would have nobody treat us. We cannot afford to put our La La La headphones on when it comes to sexual orientation and sexual identities. We have to face life's complexities head on, or the consequences are tragic.

Chapter 4

Con-version Therapy

I want to begin Chapter 4 with another story, this time from Susie in Hampshire, UK. It is actually the transcript of a vlog piece Susie recorded for me.

Susie's story

Hi,

My name's Susie and I'm 38 years old. I want to tell you why I decided to convert to homosexuality.

I wasn't always gay. I spent the first 30 years of my life living as a straight woman. As a child I played with dolls, had crushes on boys at school and male pop stars, just like all the other girls. As a teenager, I dated guys, and in my late teens, met a really nice lad at church called Paul. We started dating and when we were still going strong after university, decided to get married.

At first we were really happy. We bought a nice little house on a new build estate and set up home together. Babies followed, one of each. We were both super involved at church and though I say so myself, we were a popular couple with lots of friends. You could say we were the model Christian couple.

But then something changed in me. I couldn't pinpoint the exact moment, but I just became aware that this was all just too easy. I became dissatisfied with how good my life was. Here I was, safe, popular, happy, with the house, two kids, a husband who provided for me, and doting friends and family. But it wasn't enough. The feeling just kept gnawing away at me, this desire to be free of all this comfort and satisfaction – I called it my inner Cheshire Cat. You can have too much of a good thing, you know.

So shortly after my 30th birthday, I decided to become a lesbian. I gave it a lot of thought and prayerful reflection, but in the end it was just the obvious next step. I chatted it through with a solicitor friend first, who advised me that it would cause an enormous deal of hurt and upset, but if I was sure, he would act on my behalf.

I then broke the news to Paul that I had decided to become a lesbian. Of course, he was absolutely devastated, and made it very clear that he and the kids would have nothing more to do with me. This was an incredibly painful time for me, but I knew I had to follow through with my decision, even though I still deep down wanted to be in a relationship with a man. The kids would come round. He couldn't stop them from seeing me.

Next was my parents. This was arguably even worse. They are evangelical Christians and they told me immediately that I would burn in hell for all eternity, that my body was a temple of God and I was inviting Satan in by my decision to become a lesbian.

Then I went to see my vicar. Whilst at least he didn't shout and holler at me, the bewilderment then disgust on his face, when he realised I was serious, was almost worse. I was banned from ever setting foot in the building again. A church meeting was held, in which the congregation were told of my decision to convert to homosexuality. My life was the church and after that, I lost all my friends.

I had nowhere to go, as all my friends and family had rejected me. I couldn't even see my kids. I spent the first few weeks at a hostel. At that stage, I still had my looks, as life had been easy and good to me thus far. A few guys tried to come onto me at the hostel, and at first it was hard to resist, because deep down, I was still straight. I wanted to have sex with these guys, if only just to scratch an itch. But no, I had to be true to my decision.

I managed to get a part-time job at a leisure centre and met a nice lady at a tennis club I joined. Gradually my new life as a lesbian started to come together. I'm in a relationship with another woman now and we have our own place. It's going ok, though the sex doesn't come naturally, because obviously I'm straight really. Though things are gradually getting better, it has been absolute hell, especially the rejection of my family and friends. I rarely seen the kids, who are now teenagers, and my parents still do not talk to me. I've visibly aged – people usually think I'm way older than I am – and it's taken a massive toll on my mental health.

However, I don't regret the path I've taken. I'm glad I decided to convert to homosexuality and became a lesbian. If you are simply bored of being safe, popular and accepted by everyone, you can convert, too. Cos life can be too easy, you know? You can have too much of a good thing.

By now, you will hopefully have realised that this story is actually a spoof, and Susie is a figment of my imagination. But this is, in all seriousness, how some church leaders and church members view LGBT – as a perverse choice made by rational adults who have suddenly taken leave of their senses and left their moral compass behind at the last service station.

Conversion Therapy in the UK and beyond

It saddens me to say, as a UK citizen, that conversion therapy is still legal in my home country as I write (June 2020). LibDem MP, Layla Moran, has tabled an urgent motion in Parliament to have this practice banned, and hopefully there will be no further delays. In the USA, conversion therapy remains legal in all but 20 states, and in all but one in Australia (Victoria being the notable exception). In the European Union, a majority of 435 to 109 representatives in the European Parliament passed a resolution condemning conversion therapy in March 2018 and in so doing, urged all European Union member states to ban the practice. However, as of June 2020, conversion therapy is only *de jure* illegal in Malta, Germany, Albania and within some regions of Spain.

So, what exactly is conversion therapy? Also known as reparative therapy, it is generally described as a pseudoscientific practice aimed at changing an individual's sexual orientation, usually from homosexual to heterosexual, via psychological and/or spiritual interventions. There is no reliable scientific evidence that a person can change their sexual orientation by subjecting themselves to such interventions and thus the practice is generally frowned upon by medical institutions. However, while only 8% of Americans believed conversion therapy to be effective in 2014, the practice still receives widespread support (up to 75%) in some sectors of the populace, probably in those states where homosexuality and LGBT people are used as a political football in the interests of furthering right-wing agendas.

A brief history of conversion therapy

Ever since Sigmund Freud started his psychoanalytic practice in Vienna in the late 19th century, attempts have been made to 'cure' people of same-sex attraction and transgenderism, with methods ranging from hypnosis to barbaric practices such as testicle transplant (yes, really), lobotomization, electro shock therapy and painful injections. Freud's own psychoanalytic attempts to change the sexual orientation of his patients were actually a 'progression' from the attempts of fellow countryman, Eugen Steinach, who attempted to 'cure' men of homoerotic behaviours by transplanting testicles from heterosexual men. This project unsurprisingly failed, as the immune systems of the men in question rejected the transplanted glands.

At the turn of the 19th century, a German psychiatrist, Albert von Schrenk-Notzing, claimed at a hypnosis conference to have 'turned a gay man straight.' This was done via 45 hypnosis sessions and a few trips to a brothel, where allegedly through hypnosis, the man's sexual impulses were manipulated and diverted towards a lasting desire for women. This possibly marks the start of conversion therapy as we know it today.

Methods used

Just some of the known methods used to 'cure' men and women (but mainly men) of homosexuality are listed in the pages that follow. If we consider that many of these methods have been approved or *not disapproved of* by church leaders (we return to our equally damaging sins of commission and omission), we may quite reasonably argue again that the church has blood on its hands.

Historical Physical Methods

Ice-pick lobotomies.

This involved inserting an ice-pick above the eyeball of a person and moving it back and forth across the frontal lobe of the brain.

Chemical castration

Now only used to treat certain hormone related cancers, such as prostate cancer, chemical castration was previously used to reduce testosterone and sexual impulses in sex offenders – including gay men, who were categorised as such before the legalisation of homosexuality. This hormonal treatment, used by the infamous Danish doctor and SS Officer, Carl Vaernet, was also offered the British code-breaker Alan Turing, in lieu of a custodial sentence. Turing infamously accepted this deal from the British Government in 1952, having been found guilty of indecent homosexual acts. It had a severe psychological and physical effect on Turing and he took his own life two years afterwards at the age of just 41. This event was dramatized to powerful effect in the 2014 film *The Imitation Game* starring Benedict Cumberbatch as Alan Turing.

Electric shock

Electric shock treatment was one of several 'aversion therapies' aimed at conditioning 'the patient' to consciously or subconsciously associate pain or sickness with homosexual feelings and thereby block them out. It applied electric shocks to the hands or genitals whenever a person had a positive sexual response to an image shown on a slide.

Another variation of this involved implanting electrodes directly to the brain and administering electric shocks this way. This was pioneered by New Orleans psychiatrist, Robert Galbraith Heath, who used this form of brain stimulation in conjunction with hired prostitutes and heterosexual pornography to attempt to change the sexual orientation of gay men. Interestingly, the main criticism of his work at that time, was that it was *methodologically* unsound!

Emetic drugs

This involved giving nausea-inducing drugs to a patient whilst showing them homo-erotic imagery, including photos of their own lovers, so that they would associate unpleasant sensations and disgust with homosexuality. This was again with a view to conditioning the person to reject feelings of same-sex attraction at a conscious or subconscious level.

Masturbatory reconditioning.

The 'patient' was here encouraged to self-pleasure while watching heterosexual 'stimuli' with the aim of creating a positive association between pleasure and heterosexual acts.

The Stonewall Effect

The Stonewall Riots, where members of the New York LGBT community clashed with the police outside the Stonewall Inn in New York in 1969, led to increased focus on LGBT rights in the late 1960s and early 1970s. In 1973, following pressure from the Gay Rights Movement, but also from psychiatrists and other medical practitioners, the American Psychiatric Association (APA) removed homosexuality as a mental illness from the *Diagnostic and Statistical Manual of Mental Disorders*. Their decision was also based on empirical evidence from the likes of sexologist Alfred Kinsey and psychiatrist Evelyn Hooker.

However, when medical professionals began to eschew physical aversion techniques, faith-based groups filled the resulting void, offering 'conversion' or 'reparative therapy.' Such outfits became known as 'ex-gay ministries' and I had the misfortune to engage with some of these organisations in the late 1980s, early 1990s when I was struggling with my own sexuality, as a teenager who had recently converted to Christianity.

The mushrooming of LGBT rights groups provoked an equally strong counter-reaction from Christian groups and other self-proclaimed 'experts' in the field of sexual orientation conversion. A prominent figure in the field of conversion therapy was Joseph Nicolosi, who published *Reparative Therapy of Male Homosexuality* in 1991. In 1992 Nicolosi, along with Benjamin Kaufman and Charles Socarides, set up *The National Association for Research & Therapy of Homosexuality* (NARTH) which had as one of its aims to 'make effective psychological therapy available to all homosexual men and women who seek change.'[15]

---

[15] A good history of reparative therapy is offered by Thomas Waidzuna: Waidzunas, T., 2015. *The straight line: How the fringe science of ex-gay therapy reoriented sexuality*. University of Minnesota Press.

The organisation changed its name to the less contentious *Alliance for Therapeutic Choice and Scientific Integrity* in 2014. However, it still offers reparative therapy, judging by the mission statement on its homepage:

> *A multi-disciplinary professional and scientific organization dedicated to preserving the right of individuals to obtain the services of a therapist who honours their values, advocating for integrity and objectivity in social science research, and ensuring that competent licensed, professional assistance is available for persons who experience unwanted homosexual attractions.*[16]

But there is little integrity, based on available evidence (e.g. that of historian Elise Chenier[17]), in claiming sexual orientation can be changed through psychotherapy.

More recent psychological therapies

As indicated above, 'talk' and visualisation therapies have replaced physical interventions. However, less barbaric, psychological tactics are arguably no less

---

[16] See https://www.therapeuticchoice.com/
[17] See https://www.history.com/news/gay-conversion-therapy-origins-19th-century

harmful that their physical antecedents, and - in some cases - may well leave longer lasting damage on individuals.

Gay conversion camps & Pray the Gay Away

Conversion camps, of the type seen in 2018 films *Boy Erased* and *The Miseducation of Cameron Post* are usually run by right-wing Christian evangelical movements. At such camps, young people are isolated from family, friends and all outside influences, and subjected to 'healing prayer' – sometimes even prayers of exorcism to remove the evil spirit of homosexuality – with the aim of convincing them that homosexuality is unnatural and against God's plan. I have myself been subjected to such prayers at a well-known charismatic Christian conference held annually in the south west of the UK.

Gender Realignment

Often, as is seen to disturbingly brilliant effect in *Boy Erased*, young people are coached to perform their 'proper God-given gender role.' One 'classic' of this era, as mentioned earlier, is Nicolosi's

Reparative Therapy of Male Homosexuality[18]. In this book, the author gives the following 11 Step Plan for heterosexual conditioning:

1. Participate in sports and other manly activities
2. Avoid museums, opera, symphonies, and other non-manly activities
3. Avoid women except for romantic contact
4. Mimic the ways heterosexual men walk, talk, and interact
5. Attend church and join a men's group
6. Attend reparative therapy groups to discuss progress and/or slips back into homosexuality
7. Become more assertive with women through flirting
8. Begin heterosexual dating
9. Engage in heterosexual intercourse
10. Enter heterosexual marriage
11. Father children

The damage caused by the latter two steps in particular has become all too familiar in recent years, with many taking their own lives when 'treatment' inevitably failed. Sexual abuse of the 'clients' of such conversion therapists was also rife

---

[18] Nicolosi, J., 1997. *Reparative therapy of male homosexuality: A new clinical approach.* Jason Aronson.

during this dark psychological period, fuelled by the HIV/AIDS crisis of the mid-1980s.

I am myself somebody who entered heterosexual marriage and was encouraged to procreate on the advice of church leaders, when I confessed my same sex attraction to them back in the early 1990s.

Evidence that any of these 'reparative' techniques worked, beyond the biased claims of right-wing Christian groups, remained non-existent. There is a large body of work freely available online which charts the desperate plights of many men and women who subjected themselves/were subjected by parents and church leaders, to this dangerous form of manipulation. It is quite unbelievable to think this was all going on just over twenty years ago, and still does in some parts of the world. When Nicolosi was writing this book, I had been married one year already and was just about to start my family. Such practices feel like something from the Dark Ages!

Counselling is another form of reparative therapy still widely practised in the USA in particular, but also in Europe (predominantly Eastern Europe), as my own research participants clearly demonstrate (Shepherd, 2020b).

Into the 21st century

In 2001, United States Surgeon General, David Satcher, published a report which stated "there is no valid scientific evidence that sexual orientation can be changed."[19] That very same year, a psychiatrist by the name of Robert Spitzer claimed that reparative therapy could work on highly motivated, predominantly homosexual people who wished to become predominantly heterosexual. He based his claims on structured interviews with 200 self-selected participants, of which just over 70% were male. However, Spitzer apologised to the LGBT community in 2012, stating his findings were actually unproven. He acknowledged the study's connection to the Christian ex-gay movement, admitting that 93% of the sample were involved in church functions of one kind or another and therefore felt pressure, either internally or externally, to change their sexual orientation.

A 2002 report by Ariel Shidlo and Michael Schroeder (peer-reviewed this time), with a similar number of respondents, found that 88% of participants had failed to see any long-term change in their sexual behaviour. Three per cent claimed to

---

[19] See https://www.nytimes.com/2001/06/29/us/surgeon-general-s-report-calls-for-sex-education-beyond-abstinence.html

have changed their orientation to straight, with the remaining 9% losing sexual drive or practising celibacy with no change in directional attraction. Many of the respondents reported after-effects from the research study, such as depression, suicide ideation and attempts, and social isolation. All but one of those who claimed success in changing their orientation were ex-gay leaders or counsellors and therefore had a vested interest in making such proclamations.

Ex-gay ministries are gradually becoming discredited, as more and more failed attempts at conversion and distressing after-effects are reported. Exodus International, the umbrella organisation in control of many of the well-known ex-gay/conversion ministries globally, closed down in 2013 after nearly 40 years, when its president, Alan Chambers, acknowledged that it was impossible to change somebody's sexual orientation.

In the UK, Jeremy Marks of Courage had realised this back in 2000, when the Courage Trust infamously changed direction, from an ex-gay ministry to a fully affirming ministry for gay Christians, having the courage itself to admit that its conversion rates were zero and that the ministry was doing infinitely more harm than good.

Outlawing conversion therapy in the State of California in 2012, Governor Jerry Brown stated: 'These practices have no basis in science or medicine and they will now be relegated to the dustbin of quackery.'[20]

Sadly, "Pray the Gay Away" style counselling and psychotherapy is still very much alive and kicking in both the Western and Eastern Christian churches as accounts from my own research projects show.

Evidence of abusive clergy and church practices

As I stated earlier, I'm an academic researcher as well as an author and public speaker. While my research focuses specifically on the bisexual Christian experience, the stories I'm sharing are equally applicable, wherever you sit on the LGBT spectrum.

During a field trip to the United States in 2017, I interviewed several young people and college students about their experiences of conversion therapy and 'healing prayer.'

Liz, an 18 year old student from Tennessee explained to me how religious organisations

---

[20] See https://www.history.com/news/gay-conversion-therapy-origins-19th-century

generally operated in a covert manner concerning their real intentions, commenting:

> They're not going to call it conversion therapy, that's not how these things work… they just say the word 'talking'; they say the word 'counselling.' So they phrase it more casual than it is.

Liz went on to describe her experiences as a bisexual teenager:

> My parents… they're extremely conservative Christians… when they found out, they had a very negative reaction and they decided to send me to conversion therapy. And they thought this was the ultimate downfall of my faith, which is a common view among Christians… Basically they immediately went to my youth pastor, who'd watched me grow up… and they were like, hey, Liz has gone down a wrong path, whatever. So he was basically my therapist. So I would go about two to three times a week for about a month and a half to two months… Day One would be like Step One, and he would

like, 'Okay, so do you realise that what you're doing is wrong? Do you realise that this is a sin? … Have you read Leviticus?... At first, I was only allowed to go to school and like nothing else… no association with my friends, including a separate church… and then they took away my car, they went through my cell-phone and took that away – so basically cut off my communication with all my friends… it just kept getting worse. My dad would drive me to school every day and talk to me every day about how disgusting and awful and sinful and whatever it was. So every single day I was getting this negative, awful, you know… I would cry every morning before going to school and it just got worse and worse and worse.

Liz went on to describe how she decided to reinvent herself as a model daughter, to avoid more sanctions against her and to continue her college studies, whilst remaining bisexual at heart.

Melissa, 19, another student from Tennessee, also described an extremely negative parental reaction, this time from her Catholic mother:

My mother's reaction was terrible; probably the worst possible reaction... she first began to cry heavily, when I was reading aloud to her a letter that I had written to her about falling in love with a girl. The first thing she said through her tears was, 'I will always love you, but I will *never* support this... where is your faith in this? Are you telling me this so you will go out and hold hands with her in public and not care? This is a sin. Do you think you're going to heaven?... You're never going to have children and I'm never going to have grandkids.' Her words were extremely hurtful. She continued, 'I want you to have the life God wants for you. I want you to marry a husband who will love you and cherish you.'... I told her that I am still the same person as before, still her daughter. But she looked at me so differently. She promptly said, 'I will never come around to this.'

Similar to Liz, Melissa was also taken for 'counselling' by her parents:

My mother did make me go to a counselling session with her, my step-dad and a Christian pastor. She wanted to try to heal our relationship somehow through this. The pastor tried to be a mediator, but often took the stance that I was unholy and that the love I had for my person was not okay. He made me feel that I needed to change and stop 'sinning'… it only added to my self-hate. He referenced the Bible several times and I just remember feeling so misunderstood and judged by him. This good, white, married man that didn't even know me, or my story, and had never been in my shoes, told me how my choice was so sinful. It was an awful feeling to be judged by someone like that who is Christian.

Whilst Jason (now 40) from Massachusetts had never attended conversion therapy, he described his student experiences at an all-male accountability group at a Methodist theological seminary:

Their theology in particular was that even just thinking about [sex]… any sort of sexual arousal or eroticism… just even a fleeting thought… was literally like someone pounding a spike into Christ's breast. It's all terrible. I was in an accountability group where we would sort of confess our problems and sit around praying for one another. We'd have conferences and special break-out sessions where they'd be all guys, and you'd talk through stuff, with a lot of weeping and crying. And I'd feel a tremendous guilt for masturbation and things like that. Why can't I get over this, sort of thing.

Elmo (25) from Georgia described his negative experiences with the Seventh-day Adventist Church at the time of coming out as bisexual:

I was asked to leave a Christian campus when I came out. I was 14… they asked me to leave, just for coming out. Whole families would just stop talking to us, like just done. They wouldn't even respond; they didn't even recognise we were there at church anymore. We were going to the local supermarket after I got asked to leave, and the pastor of our church at the time was there. And I said, 'Hey Pastor,' and I held my hand out to shake his hand. And he looked at my hand and he walked away from me.

During my data collection in the UK for the same doctoral study, no participants had been directly subjected to conversion therapy. However, Corinne, 41, was aware that healing prayer for homosexuality existed (as well as an appalling lack of confidentiality) at a large Anglican church in London she had attended as a student:

> There was a guy who was on the leadership team, not one of the main leaders, but on the leadership team, whom I was told in hushed tones after a service – he was pointed out as he walked around the church – in hushed tones, it was said, "He's gay, but he's praying it through. He's seeking the Lord's healing and he's not acting on it, and that's the important thing. So we're all supporting him, all praying for him, and he's seeking healing and he's going to be healed."

More recently, I have been interviewing LGBT Christians around Europe on their experiences of

pastoral provision. Alessandra (22) from Italy
replied, when asked whether she knew anyone who
had been subject to conversion therapy:

> I know someone, yes, my ex-girlfriend…
> she had parents who were more
> restrictive than mine. She challenged her
> parents about her sexuality, what she was
> going through. I remember that they sent
> her to a psychiatrist to try and kind of
> make her better. It was a general
> psychiatrist, but with the aim of curing
> her. Because they thought it was all in her
> head – 'she's a teenager, she doesn't
> know what she's doing. She just wants to
> explore.' It didn't actually work. She's
> actually transitioned now to become a
> man. She wasn't even lesbian or bisexual,
> she's trans. So, it definitely didn't work.

I asked Alessandra if, in her opinion, priests or
psychiatrists were trained to do this work.

> They're not trained and I think they use
> the Bible to kind of discriminate against
> us. And it's really upsetting, because
> what I get from the Bible is basically help
> and love each other, that's the whole

message that I get. Yes, I understand that there are rules out there, but I think that most of these rules come from having a church that is ancient and they should actually start to do something about that. Because I believe there's a lot of people out there who are getting hurt every day and it's just upsetting.

Lilo (25) from the Netherlands described her experiences at an unnamed evangelical Protestant Church:

The church where I grew up would teach us from the beginning of my youth that any non-heterosexual feeling or behaviour is a sickness. They also claimed that we can be healed from these feelings…We did have two books that contained the subject of how to cure homosexuality and how to suppress it.

Katja (46) from Switzerland spoke of the time she spent in the Vineyard Christian Fellowship prior to coming out:

I was part of an urban Vineyard Church (similar to Pentecostal) with about 1000 members (most of them between 20-40 years of age) for about 20 years. I had to leave the church when I came out as homosexual.

I asked Katja why she had felt obliged to leave the Vineyard Church:

To be out as homo- or bisexual and still be part of the church is possible just as a visitor, but you cannot participate in any leadership, or other tasks or groups, so it must feel awful to be out and still go to that church. I don't know anybody who came out and is still member of that church. It would hurt too much to be just a visitor after having been in a team and it would mean you lose probably most or all of your friends, because they would try to "convert" you back to normal, and if that did not work, they would not be your friends any longer because - as they see it - you live in constant sin. The only way that would be barely tolerated is if you come out, but then stay celibate the rest of your life, which I guess is not the heart's desire of most homo- or bisexual Christians. I came out as lesbian because I didn't realize there was such a thing as "bisexual" some 15 years ago. Since I was banned from all the groups I led, I was not keen to specify later that I might be bisexual. I just wanted to run.

How had h er Christian friends reacted to Katja coming out?

Most Christians and Christian friends I had reacted the same way. The denomination did not make a difference, but as I was only moving around in charismatic churches, I don't know about traditional churches. They said they still loved me, but they couldn't love my sinful choice. For them, that meant I could - and would have to - change to stay their friend. As in my heart I knew this would not be possible (after trying for several years even with professional help), I knew I would lose those friends, which was the case. Of all the friendships I had, only two have lasted until now. I even had two talks with my senior pastor about my sexual orientation and the slogan of the church that they accept everyone, but the result didn't change.

The fact remains that in 2020, only three countries in the whole of Europe – Albania, Germany and Malta – have legally outlawed conversion therapy, which includes talk therapies and not just barbaric physical aversion therapies.

I have noticed that when typing 'conversion therapy,' predictive texting often amends it to conversation therapy. Perhaps this is prophetic. Because it is **conversation** that is needed and it is conversation, not conversion, that is therapeutic, more than anything. Sharing of lived experiences in dialogue with others, particular those who make and shape rules in our church hierarchies, is what is needed, not shaming and screwing up vulnerable individuals, often to the extent that victims never recover from such humiliating experiences, even leading some to tragically take their own lives. It is not sufficient to claim lack of personal involvement. When there is a food shortage - even if it doesn't affect our own congregation - we collect for the Basics Bank. Where there is a shortage of love and common decency, churches should also step in, whoever the victim is - or leaders and congregants have blood on their hands.

Chapter 5

What would Jesus do?

The answer to this question is, frankly, I don't know. And neither do any of us. However, I can hazard a guess, based on the available evidence, which is all any of us can realistically do.

I once saw a cartoon by a very talented biblical scholar turned cartoonist in the United States, called David Heyward, aka the Naked Pastor. I can't recall the exact wording, but it went something like this. Jesus says to the Pharisees, "You use Scripture to understand love, I use love to understand Scripture." In other words, Jesus approaches Scripture through the lens of love, Scripture serves his goal of love, rather than love is defined by Scripture. For Jesus, the Pharisees were putting the cart before the horse. They were saying, you can only love, or you can only serve, or you can only wear those clothes or eat that food, if it says so in Scripture – rather than 'how might we understand this or that passage based on the unerring fact that Jesus is love because he is the son and reflection of God, who is love.' (see John 1:14) It is more than contextual Bible study. It is love-centred Bible study.

To me, there are obvious parallels between the legalistic Pharisees in the Bible and faith leaders who reject LGBT people, particularly on the evangelical wing of the Western Christian Church and the Orthodox wing of the Eastern Christian Church. And it's not just rejection of LGBT people, but rejection of anyone who does not fit their prescription of what a well-behaved God-fearing Christian might look like. As a divorced mother of three, currently in a relationship with a woman, I am on the highway to hell, by their standards. Fortunately, God's Spirit is alive and well in my heart, and I feel the peace that transcends understanding since my own personal rebirth at the ripe old age of 45. I am, frankly, a far nicer person to be around than I ever was when I was toeing the line at church, in the mistaken idea that I was being 'godly' by pretending to be someone I was not and slashing my own soul in two (not to mention the impact on all those directly and indirectly affected by my lack of congruence as a human being).

There appears to me to be two paths you can take when approaching the issue of homosexuality in the Bible. The popular path, the one taken by most affirming and non-affirming Christians alike, is what a guy called Tim Kochs once called 'a pissing contest' between male theologians.[21] It involves taking the so-called seven "Clobber Passages" (or "Texts of Terror") on homosexuality in the Bible and dissecting them. Does this word mean homosexual, or effeminate? Is it talking about homosexual acts with men or angels? Is it about pagan idolatry or homosexuality? Does this word mean pederasty or penetrative sex? And so on and so forth.

Biblical scholars on the affirming or non-affirming side of the debate will then argue back and forth about the precise meaning of lone words in Ancient Hebrew and Greek.

Key biblical figures are then subjected to a tug of war of cultural appropriation, with poor King David frequently the central marker on the rope between the Traditionalist and Affirming teams. For the traditionalists, David is a sword-wielding testosterone fuelled hero, lauded for his faithful diehard friendship with Jonathan. For the LGBT affirming team, he's Scripture's gay icon, rejecting women for the greater love of a man. A similar game is played with Ruth, distant ancestor of Jesus himself. Is she the faithful daughter-in-law and canny charmer of Boaz, or a lesbian role model,

---

[21] See Koch, T. R. (2001). A homoerotic approach to Scripture. *Theology and Sexuality, 7*(14), 10-22.

shacking up with her ex-mother in law and bringing up a child in their sapphic love-nest?

The fact is, *we don't know*. The Bible was written a very long time ago, based on a largely oral tradition. It has been subject to endless rewrites and redactions. It abounds with translational anomalies and was written in a patriarchal society where men ruled and women's stories were largely discounted. It was also written in a time where none of the scientific knowledge we have today existed. The New Testament, for example, takes place largely in Roman times, where a physician called Galen taught that women were simply inferior biological versions of men. Galen believed that the uterus and fallopian tubes in women were simply internalised penises and testicles that had not dropped. If you think of the shape of a womb and fallopian tubes, you get the picture. Today that seems blatantly ridiculous, because human biology and genetics tells us this is not the case. But in those days, that was accepted scientific knowledge.

There are endless biblical scholars, some more scholarly than others, who argue the case back and forth as to the precise meaning of the seven passages in Scripture. Gagnon, John Smith, Vines, Sharpe, Helminiak - I could go on for a long time. I have a PhD in this stuff. It's boring and it entirely misses the point. We do not apply this same principles to other lifestyle issues in Scripture that clearly apply to an entirely different type of society to the one we live in today. If you really want to have your mind opened by the various translational anomalies these passages offer, I heartily recommend the comprehensive body of work of K Renato Lings, <u>Love Lost in Translation</u>.

For now, to satisfy those of you who would like some contextual information clarified succinctly, Table 5.1 lists these seven so-called 'texts of terror' or 'clobber passages' typically used by fundamentalist/conservative evangelical Christians to deny support to LGBT people. This table, reproduced with the kind permission of <u>www.religioustolerance.org</u>, an Ontario based consultancy for religious tolerance, gives an overview of the standard interpretation of the most common Scriptures used to discuss same-sex attraction in the Church, from both a fundamentalist and progressive position. (Please refer to **Appendix 1** to read the actual Bible quotes, as this table does not reproduce the Scriptural passages). The strength and integrity of this particular table lies in the ecumenical basis of the organisation, which is not affiliated to a particular denomination, but rather seeks to reach consensus on disputatious areas of theology via multi-faith direction and scholarship.

Table 5.1: The 'Clobber Passages'

Location	Typical interpretation by religious conservatives	Typical interpretation by religious progressives & secularists
Genesis 19	Condemns all same-sex sexual behaviour, whether by two men, two women, within a loving committed relationship or a 'one-night stand.'	Condemns anal raping of strangers for the purpose of humiliation.
Leviticus 18:22	Condemns all same-sex sexual behaviour.	Condemns gay ritual sex in a Pagan temple and/or males having sex in a woman's bed.
Leviticus 20:13	Condemns all same-sex sexual behaviour.	Condemns gay ritual sex in a temple and/or males having sex in a woman's bed.
Romans 1:26-27	Condemns all homosexual behaviour as unnatural.	Describes a group of heterosexuals who, against their basic nature, engage in same-sex behaviour during ritual orgies.
1 Corinthians 6:9-10	Sexually active homosexuals will go to hell, not heaven, at death. Once truly	Male child molesters and the children they molest will go to Hell, not Heaven, at death.

	saved, homosexuals will become heterosexuals.	
1 Timothy 1:9- 10	Condemns all same-sex sexual behaviour.	Refers to child molesters and the children they molest.
Jude 1:7	Sexually active homosexuals will go to hell, not heaven, at death.	Humans who have sex with other species -- angels in this case -- will go to Hell, not Heaven, at death.

Reproduced by kind permission of www.religioustolerance.org

The table demonstrates the potential differences in interpretation when these passages are placed in the cultural context of the time, where hospitality and purity laws were literally written in stone and pagan temple rituals had infiltrated the fledgling Christian communities in today's Italy, Greece and Turkey.

There was, as we can see, no concept of sexual orientation or loving homosexual relationships, simply sexual acts that were acceptable or not acceptable for people of God in the context of the culture at that time.

Thus, it can be seen that there is a spectrum of interpretations of the salient passages of Scripture on homosexuality, from contextual readings of the

Bible by the liberal left wing of the global church, to literal readings from the fundamentalist right.

There are actually ten passages on homosexuality in my list in **Appendix 1** but the seven above are the commonly quoted texts in the homosexuality debate in the church.

The Woody Approach

The second path, and in my view, by far the more fruitful, is what I call the woody approach. This has nothing to do with Toy Story. The woody approach is the approach I use - and I don't actually know any other affirming LGBT biblical scholars who use this - though David Heyward appears to in his cartoons. But I'm sure there must be some out there.

Why the 'woody' approach? Quite simply, you need to be able to see the wood for the trees. The wood is Jesus, light of the world and human representation or incarnation of the love of God. The trees are all that other stuff: Scripture, tradition, church, Christian subculture. When we get bogged down in precise meanings of a relatively insignificant number of passages on one subject, we are hugging trees, sometimes strangling the life out of them, instead of seeing the wood, the bigger picture.

At this point, you may be up in arms or at least slightly uneasy that I've lumped Scripture in there. But going back to that cartoon, Scripture is to serve the greater goal of spreading the Gospel of Christ, not to be idolised in its own form. If I gave you a choice:- read my autobiography or meet me for coffee and ask me lots of questions, which would tell you more about me? For one thing, my autobiography might have been written ten years ago and not tell you all that's happened since. Secondly, how much more of the person is revealed through a live encounter? Jesus is alive and dynamic; Scripture is illuminating and inspiring but no replacement for an encounter with the living God, whom we find in our hearts and minds and in our guts by virtue of the Holy Spirit. And the Bible was written a long time ago, subject to interpretative and translational inconsistencies, at a time where half the population was barely acknowledged and scientific knowledge was minimal. It was written at a time when women had to stay in a tent for a week if they had their period and people could not wear mixed fabrics.

Those Christians who take a position against LGBT people based on ancient purity laws from Leviticus – have you ever seen them protesting outside Primark in the UK or Target in the US about people wearing polyester? A pastor might enquire why his congregation is abnormally low that Sunday. "Well, Pastor Thomas, it's because the women in the congregation are all in sync now and we have 32 off with their period. We might get half back for Wednesday night home group…"

So when we get hung up on what is meant by Leviticus 18: 22 or Romans 1, are we doing so out of genuine concern for breaking God's laws or is something different going on? If you're going to nit-pick, at least be consistent about it. I would suggest there is a considerable degree of 'sin deflection' or speck removal going on here.

Back to my woody approach:- personally, I think where we're going wrong, is in playing non-affirming LGBT scholars at their own game. And in so doing, we become a little legalistic and Pharisaical as well, also focusing on the trees, all seven of them. I'm aware of the kind of Matthew Vine[22] argument, namely you need to speak the language of evangelical Christians and engage with biblical exegesis on the homosexual issue. But based on my own experience, I disagree. It's like arguing politics with your parents. Exhausting, frustrating and unlikely to yield results. Take Brexit, for example… no, let's not.

---

[22] See Vines, M., 2014. *God and the gay Christian: The biblical case in support of same-sex relationships*. Convergent.

We need to get people to see the wood, not focus on the trees. And the wood is the love of God over all of his or her creation, manifest in Christ. And that overarching love is revealed in Scripture. But we also need to have a woody approach to Scripture, not focusing on individual trees, lest we lose our way in the forest.

Most Christians agree that Jesus is the ultimate expression of love. I don't buy into atonement theory – it is not consonant with a loving God in my view, but that's another argument for another day - but I do believe Jesus died and rose again and that he came to earth to model God's love for all people. In my head and in my heart and in my gut, I am totally convinced that Paul was right in Romans 8:38 when he said nothing can separate us from the love of God. I also know in my head, heart and gut, that the Jesus who consorted with lowly women, who mixed with beggars and disabled people, would in no way reject anyone for something they could do absolutely nothing about, i.e. their sexuality. If he did, I am sure there would be a negative mention of homosexuality in one of the four gospels or a parable that clearly alludes to same-sex relationships. As it is, there is no mention, though a case can be made for the homosexual credentials of the centurion's lover who is healed in Luke 7, or the eunuchs Jesus refers to in Matthew

19 being transgendered people or gay men. Cases have even been made for Jesus himself being potentially gay based on the references to the Beloved Disciple, but that's a whole new debate in itself – and not one I feel qualified to lead.

Now, if you are listening to this and you genuinely are not sure whether same-sex attraction or transgender identity actually exists, can I just assure you, *it does*. I struggled most of my adult life to deny my same-sex attraction. It does not go away, *ever*; it was always there and always will be. To deny it is akin to denying my eyes are grey-green. I can put coloured contact lenses on, but it doesn't change the colour of my eyes underneath. And to deny who I am in my very essence is to say God got me wrong. And I did that for most of my adult life and it made me ill, very ill, and I hurt a lot of people. And I cannot believe that such a torturous existence is a God of love's will for me or for anyone else in my situation.

The woody approach is about seeing the bigger picture, about recognising the overriding love of Jesus. Jesus did not reject anyone. The only people that appeared to annoy him were the Pharisees. Why? Because they missed the point. With their legalistic nit-picking of his every move and their constant attempts to trip Jesus up, they entirely misunderstood his message. We see this time and time again in Scripture, where Jesus is accused of breaking the rules. In Luke 6, Jesus and the disciples get a bit hungry while they're out and about. They crush some grain in a field and eat it, the biblical equivalent of grabbing a quick bowl of Weetabix to keep the hunger at bay. But the Pharisees catch wind of this and tick Jesus off for harvesting the field on the Sabbath. Harvesting the field? They only picked some grain to eat, for goodness sake. It's a little bit like insinuating someone in a loving monogamous homosexual relationship is engaging in mass orgies with Satanists on the Sabbath.

We find another example later in this passage from Luke 6, where Jesus heals the hand of a leper in the synagogue. Not only does Jesus touch the hand of an unclean person, Jesus is also well and truly ticked off by the Pharisees and scribes for healing on the Sabbath, in church of all places! But Jesus replies that clearly the need to love and heal comes before rules and regulations. As Jesus says in Mark 2:27-28, "The Sabbath was made for man, not man for the Sabbath." Rules are there to serve you, not the other way round. **Love** rules (= love takes precedence over rules), not love **rules** (= worship rules). Again, they cannot see the wood for the trees and put the cart before the horse and other metaphors of this ilk.

There are many more examples of Jesus breaking the rules. Forgiving sins, touching lepers, eating with social outcasts, consorting with women, turning tables over, were all against Jewish law and social convention. Jesus repeatedly told all who challenged him that love was more important than rule-keeping.

Jesus knew that the complex Jewish law was creating ridiculous burdens for people. He wanted people to be unburdened of these heavy yokes. He tells us his yoke is easy and his burden light. So he simplified the law in Matthew 22: 37-40:

"You shall **love the Lord your God** with all your heart and with all your soul and with all your mind. This is the great and first commandment. And a second is like it: You shall **love your neighbour as yourself.** On these two commandments depend all the Law and the Prophets."

When it comes to LGBT people, if you're a non-affirming straight person, please just ask yourself this:

How would you feel if somebody told you that what came entirely naturally, how you have always felt, was just *wrong*?

That you could not engage romantically or sexually with another person for the rest of your life?

That you had to settle for loneliness and abstinence all the days of your life?

Love your neighbour as yourself. Do not place burdens on your neighbour that you would not place on yourself.

There are those who compare homosexuality to child sexual abuse. They will argue that sexual abuse of children may feel natural to an abuser, but is wrong and apply this same principle to same sex attraction and activity. But that's a whole different ballgame. Child sexual abuse is about attacking vulnerable people and abuse of the weak and vulnerable is clearly outlawed by Christ. But two adults in a loving relationship, who are not hurting anyone by lying or cheating or pretending to be someone they are not – I cannot see how that goes against the essence of Christ or Christ's modelling of love **in any way**, whether we believe David and Jonathan are a homosexual coupling or not, or whether we view the centurion's servant whom Jesus heals in Luke 7 to be the guard's male partner or not (the Greek word for manservant, *pais*, is also the word for gay lover).

What is clear from the Gospels is this: we cannot please God by legalism - love and care for others take precedence. Jesus does not break the rules, in the words of Monty Python, because he is a very naughty boy[23], but because loving the individual is more important. Rules are there to serve us, but we are not here to serve the rules. Use them appropriately. Jesus is alive in and around us today through his Spirit. We can live by faith and follow the Spirit right here right now and know in our gut what Jesus would do. That's called a living faith. And just as I am convinced, as was Paul, that nothing can separate us from the love of God. I am also convinced that Jesus would *never* judge or discriminate against someone for something they could do absolutely nothing about, such as being born same-sex attracted. There are no incidences in the Bible of Jesus trying to convert a gay person, yet we know there were LGBT people in Ancient Greece and Rome, history and art tell us so. And we know that Jesus consorted with all sectors of society. It clearly just wasn't even an issue - whereas judgement of others and harshness clearly *was*.

There are arguments on all sides of the fence around the Old Testament and Pauline passages on homosexuality. As I stated earlier, that is not my

---

[23] Monty Python's Life of Brian, see
https://www.imdb.com/title/tt0079470/

preferred focus. I know all the exegetical arguments around the seven salient passages, and I can write/speak on that kind of stuff. But in my view, this is not the correct approach. Jewish exclusivity and purity laws in the Old Testament were superseded by Jesus, who accepted Gentiles or non-Jews into the fold. In terms of the New Testament, I do not read anywhere in Scripture that Paul is the son and incarnation of God and that I can only access God through Paul. I worship Jesus. And to me, it is clear as night and day that Jesus would do nothing but love and accept an LGBT person who was not cheating, lying nor hurting anyone. I know it in my head, in my heart and in my gut.

Chapter 6

Concluding Thoughts

I am sure if you've got this far that it's pretty clear where I stand on the role the church has played in the crucifixion of ~~Christ~~ LGBT Christians.

In the unlikely event you didn't quite catch it, I believe there is **nothing** about the character of Jesus and **no evidence** from Scripture to suggest he would have a problem either accepting an LGBT person or expecting them to change their sexuality. Jesus consorted with women, foreigners, eunuchs and potentially also a gay manservant in Luke 7 – as mentioned earlier, the Greek word *pais* for manservant in the healing of the Roman Centurion's attendant is the same word as male concubine. In all cases, Jesus shows these people love, kindness and respect.

Time and time again, we see Jesus *accepting people as they are*. When the Samaritan woman at the well is tenderly but firmly chastised by Jesus (John 4), it is for her unfaithfulness, not for her gender or sexuality. Jesus does not heal the centurion's servant in Luke 7 of his sexuality, if he is indeed gay, but of his physical illness. The eunuch[24] in Matthew 19 is not told to 'man up' or 'grow one.'

Unless I am reading a different Bible, I see nothing that suggests Jesus expects *anyone* to change a part of their natural character or sexual orientation; indeed we are told in Psalm 139 that God created our inmost being. In the words of Jane Clementi, mother of suicide victim, Tyler Clementi, in Chapter 2: *To try and change what God has created causes significant harm.*

To all those who still doubt that people choose to be homosexual, or bisexual, or transgender, I repeat this question:

When did you decide to be heterosexual?

To which I'd just like to add these considerations, too:

Who has ever asked you to shut down your heart, mind and soul?

And if they did, would you?

---

[24] This word also several meanings in the original Greek and could simply refer to an official. However, it is generally thought to refer to a eunuch – theologian K Renato Lings has done extensive work in this area.

Could you?

In the figure of Christ, I see a person who treated *everyone*, even those who hated him, with love, kindness and respect. Perhaps the question should be less 'what would Jesus do?' but the more tangible, what *did* Jesus do?

From the secondary evidence we have in Scripture - and I am also a Bible-based scholar - there is no indication whatsoever that Jesus Christ, the human incarnation of God, had a problem with people who loved each other faithfully and justly.

Conversely, he had every problem with hypocrites, finger-pointers, abusers of power and behaviours which target the vulnerable in society. He had no time for those who insisted on behaviours or sacrifices from others they would not demand of themselves, for example, the woman accused of adultery in John 8.

It is clear that the Pharisees come in for more criticism than any other single group in the Gospels. Who do the Pharisees more closely resemble in today's society? LGBT people in loving, self-giving romantic relationships, or fundamentalist church leaders and condemnatory Christians? It's a no-brainer.

I believe that church leaders, lay Christians, medical practitioners and politicians who have told

LGBT people, young and old, in whatever format it takes, that they are *wrong* have blood on their hands. I also believe that church leaders, lay Christians, medical practitioners and politicians who have sat back and said *nothing* about these issues have blood on their hands, in the same way those of us who sit back and let black people suffer injustice because we're white and comfortable are culpable. In the words of Martin Luther King, there's no freedom unless we're all free. There are no bystanders to injustice of any kind. As Lieutenant General David Morrison stated, following a report into bullying and harassment in the army[25]:

> *The standard you walk past is the standard you accept. That goes for all of us, but especially those who, by their rank, have a leadership role.*

In my view, there are way too many books printed on the seven clobber passages from Scripture from Christian writers on either side of the divide. It's old

---

[25] See https://www.huffingtonpost.com.au/dr-nikki-stamp/walking-past-standards_b_8181224.html?ncid=other_email_o63gt2jcad4&utm_campaign=share_email

news and I have no wish to rehash the same old material found in these. It kind of misses the point, anyway, as I stated in Chapter 5. To me, it is obvious that we cannot resort to non-contextual readings of Scripture and use the Bible as an exact roadmap for 21st century living, so it is neither here nor there what *arsenokoitai* means. I do not borrow my Dad's 1974 AA map of Britain when I'm driving to an unfamiliar place; I look it up on the GPS and consider the current road conditions.

I will take a fellow Christian seriously about literal readings of the Texts of Terror when they have rid their wardrobes of all mixed fabrics, eschewed shellfish and fled/had their wife flee to the red tent during menstruation. And even then, only if they have engaged – and I mean *truly engaged* with the issue of sexual orientation and gender identity, by listening to the experiences of those who live this reality every second, every minute, every hour, every day of their lives.

It is no coincidence – as we read in the article by Jane Clementi – that it is often only when an issue touches our own lives, that our hearts are softened to grasp reality.

Life is complex; people are complex. *And Jesus knows that and identifies with us.*

References

Brennan, D. J., Ross, L. E., Dobinson, C., Veldhuizen, S., & Steele, L. S. (2010). Men's sexual orientation and health in Canada. *Canadian Journal of Public Health/Revue Canadienne de Sante'e Publique*, 255-258.

Church of England (1991). *Issues in Human Sexuality*. Church House Publishing.

Freud, S. (1991). *On Sexuality*. London: Penguin.

Gibbs, J. J., & Goldbach, J. (2015). Religious Conflict, Sexual Identity, and Suicidal Behaviors among LGBT Young Adults. *Arch Suicide Res, 19*(4), 472-488. doi:10.1080/13811118.2015.1004476

Kinsey, A. C., Pomeroy, W. B., & Martin, C. E. (1948). Sexual behavior in the human male.

Koch, T. R. (2001). A homoerotic approach to Scripture. *Theology and Sexuality, 7*(14), 10-22.

Lings, K. R. (2013). *Love lost in translation: homosexuality and the Bible*. Trafford Publishing.

Meyer, I. H. (2003). Prejudice, social stress, and mental health in lesbian, gay, and bisexual populations: conceptual issues and research evidence. *Psychological bulletin, 129*(5), 674.

SFHRC. (2011). Bisexual Invisibility: Impacts and Recommendations. *The San Francisco Human Rights Commission.*

Shepherd, C.A. (2020a). Depression and suicidality among bisexual Christians. In A.K.T. Yip & A. Toft, (Eds), *Bisexuality, religion and spirituality: Critical perspectives.*(pp. 156-175). Abingdon: Routledge.

Shepherd, C.A. (2020b) *Bi the Way: Pastoring bisexual Christians in Europe*. UK: Easy Yoke Publishing.

Shepherd, C.A. 2018. *Bisexuality and the Western Christian Church: The Damage of Silence.* London: Palgrave MacMillan

Shepherd, C.A. 2017. *Bisexual Christians and Mental Health: Why the Church Needs to be More Welcoming.* Unpublished Doctoral Thesis, University of Winchester, UK.

Sommers, J. (2016). *119: My life as a bisexual Christian.* London: Darton, Longman & Todd.

Appendix 1

Ten passages on same-sex attraction in the Bible and an attempt at neutral summaries of them

- **Genesis 19: 4-8 - The Destruction of Sodom & Gomorrah**

  But before they lay down, the men of the city, the men of Sodom, both young and old, all the people to the last man, surrounded the house; and they called to Lot, 'Where are the men who came to you tonight? Bring them out to us, so that we may know them.' Lot went out of the door to the men, shut the door after him, and said, 'I beg you, my brothers, do not act so wickedly. Look, I have two daughters who have not known a man; let me bring them out to you, and do to them as you please; only do nothing to these men, for they have come under the shelter of my roof.'

  In this passage, the men of Sodom ask Lot if they can engage in sex with his male visitors. Lot says this is disgraceful behaviour and offers his daughters instead, as to have sex with the visitors would be a breach of hospitality for which he would be held accountable.

- **Leviticus 18: 22 - Purity Laws**

  You shall not lie with a male as with a woman; it is an abomination.

  This line from Leviticus is one of a list of purity laws that God's people must keep.

- **Leviticus 20: 13 - Purity Laws**

  If a man lies with a male as with a woman, both of them have committed an abomination; they shall be put to death; their blood is upon them.

  As above.

- **Ruth 1: 16-17 - Ruth & Naomi**

  But Ruth said, 'Do not press me to leave you or to turn back from following you! Where you go, I will go; where you lodge, I will lodge; your people shall be my people, and your God my God. Where you die, I will die— there will I be buried. May the Lord do thus and so to me, and more as well, if even death parts me from you!'

  In this passage, Ruth refuses to return to her own people on the death of her husband, as was common practice, and clings to her mother-in-law, Naomi. She makes a pact to stay with Naomi forever.

- **1 Samuel 18: 1 - David & Jonathan**

  When David had finished speaking to Saul, the soul of Jonathan was bound to the soul of David, and Jonathan loved him as his own soul.

  This passage describes the deep mutual love felt instantly between David and King Saul's son, Jonathan.

- **2 Samuel 1: 26 - David & Jonathan**

  I am distressed for you, my brother Jonathan; greatly beloved were you to me; your love to me was wonderful, passing the love of women.

  David is about to go to battle and knows he is unlikely to see Jonathan again.

- **Romans 1: 26-27 - Paul's Letter to the Church in Rome**

  For this reason God gave them up to degrading passions. Their women exchanged natural intercourse for unnatural, and in the same way also the men, giving up natural intercourse with women, were consumed with passion for one another. Men committed shameless acts with men and received in their own persons the due penalty for their error.

The Apostle Paul expresses his views on immoral sexual expression in his letter to the Christian church in Rome.

- **1 Corinthians 6: 9-10 - Paul's Letter to the Church in Corinth**

Do you not know that wrongdoers will not inherit the kingdom of God? Do not be deceived! Fornicators, idolaters, adulterers, male prostitutes, sodomites, thieves, the greedy, drunkards, revilers, robbers—none of these will inherit the kingdom of God.

The Apostle Paul tells the church in Corinth what sort of behaviour excludes people from God's kingdom.

- **1 Timothy 1: 8-11 - Paul's Letter to Timothy**

Now we know that the law is good, if one uses it legitimately. This means understanding that the law is laid down not for the innocent but for the lawless and disobedient, for the godless and sinful, for the unholy and profane, for those who kill their father or mother, for murderers, fornicators, sodomites, slave traders, liars, perjurers, and whatever else is contrary to the sound teaching that conforms to the glorious gospel of the blessed God, which he entrusted to me.

Here the Apostle Paul is explaining to the young leader, Timothy, what sort of behaviours are deemed lawless according to the Gospel.

- **Jude 1: 7 - The Epistle of Jude**

Likewise, Sodom and Gomorrah and the surrounding cities, which, in the same manner as they, indulged in sexual immorality and pursued unnatural lust, serve as an example by undergoing a punishment of eternal fire.

This passage suggests that all peoples and cities which engage in sexual immorality will face eternal damnation, based on Old Testament events at Sodom and Gomorrah.

About the author

Carol A Shepherd is an author, college lecturer and LGBT faith activist from Eastleigh, near Southampton, UK. You can find her books at www.carolshepherdbooks.info

If you valued this book, the author would greatly appreciate a review on Amazon to spread the word. You can also subscribe to Carol's newsletter, The Bi Christian Writer https://www.subscribepage.com/bichristianwriter

More titles from Easy Yoke Publishing can be found at www.easyyoke.org

Printed in Poland
by Amazon Fulfillment
Poland Sp. z o.o., Wrocław